D1564547

The
Devil's
Child

Books by Fleda Brown Jackson

Fishing With Blood
Do Not Peel The Birches

Fleda Brown Jackson

The
Devil's
Child

1975   1999
Twenty-Five Years of Publishing
Carnegie Mellon University Press

Acknowledgments

Some of the poems in this book have been printed, in other versions (and often in groups), in *Mid-American Review, New Virginia Review, Shenandoah, Sycamore Review, West Branch,* and *Yarrow*. "Burdett Palmer's Foot," in another version, won the James Wright Prize for Vol. XI of *Mid-American Review*. (That previous version also appears in *Do Not Peel the Birches*, Purdue University Press, 1993).

This book owes a great deal to the close reading and encouragement of Jeanne Murray Walker, Dabney Stuart, Margaret Gibson, Donald Hall, Cruce Stark, Pamela Stewart, Mary Rose Callaghan, Anne Colwell, Susan Goodman, and, as ever and always, Jerry Beasley. I am, of course, particularly grateful to W. D. Snodgrass for generously contributing the Foreword. I am also grateful to the several friends and colleagues who supplied me with information about the Catholic Church and about multiple personality disorder. And finally, I wish to thank the University of Delaware for a sabbatical leave during which I was able to revise this manuscript.

This book is dedicated to the real Barbara, and to Kathryn.

Foreword

Readers who know Fleda Brown Jackson's earlier books—*Fishing With Blood* and *Do Not Peel the Birches*—may well wonder who wrote this one. Those earlier books clearly reflect the qualities that I (like others who know her) associate with Fleda: intelligence, reasonability, warmth, good humor. This book opens to a collision between pietistic quotations from the *New Baltimore Catechism* on one hand and, on the other, a history recounted by a certain Barbara who sees herself as the devil's child and her life as one long entanglement in nearly unspeakable evils.

Snowed in together after a church meeting, Barbara tells Suzanna—a writer who also attends this church—of being raised in a Satanic cultist family, subject not only to abuse, violent and sexual, but also to engagement in barbarous rites and ceremonies. This has entailed not only defilement and sexual violation (first by her father) but also obscene parodies of crucifixion which lead to animal or human sacrifices and cannibalism. Later, Barbara has been shared as a sexual slave by her father and her equally abusive husband, then has subjected her daughter to a lesser abomination. Enduring such conditions, Barbara has devised multiple personalities for herself: Sarah, who coolly relays Barbara's story; Martha, who is invisible; Mike, tougher and able to fight back; Patty, the angelic and well-loved "sunshine" child; still another character whose only name is "Me."

The story is told with a fascinating subliterate command:

> Every night
> I opened my heart to God
> as quietly as a fern . . .

or again:

> Just
> before a man dies, he turns sober
> as a judge, and I can tell you
> fear has a smell that comes through
> even alcohol . . .
> They leave him nothing to see

with, or talk with . . .
They take off everything
he can live without.

Even as she describes this ferocious family, a related but benign
family is forming around her with Suzanna and the priest, Father
Andrew, as surrogate parents. And Barbara has at least as much effect
on them as they on her.

Suzanna, expectably, stands in part for the author herself.
Yet there are significant differences: the author, for the poem's
purposes, has split herself into three characters (Barbara, Suzanna
and Father Andrew); Suzanna has kept herself whole by a kind of
meliorism: "I keep moving [Barbara's] words to safety . . . I have not
believed in evil." If Barbara has seen too much savage wrong,
Suzanna has tried to see none.

Re-awakened to cruelty and evil, she finds a disturbing
parallel between Barbara's scenes of torture "upstairs" and a favorite
childhood game of her own. She and her younger sister loved to
crouch under the bedcovers, giggling with fright as their father
would sneak up the creaking stairs then "pounce on the covers with a
horrible roar . . . 'It's the Grammash,' he'd growl." Why should
children, free of any actual threat or danger, enjoy pretending to be
attacked, enjoy picturing their obviously benign father as a monster?
Is this merely a reassurance that one can survive attacks? Or may
this point to something demonic rooted in human families and
human psyches?

Barbara's problems have also highlighted and clarified
Father Andrew's. The recognition of human differences and of
others' power and cruelty—what Suzanna has tried to ignore—led
Barbara to split and divide her personality, to become smaller and
less visible. Father Andrew, instead, has accreted more and more to
himself, compulsively eating, taking on the weighty role of priest and
an identity with the Church. Again, though Father Andrew becomes
only marginally aware of this, the reader must notice a direct, if
inverted, relation between the church's rites—especially the taking
on of the body and blood of the sacrificial saviour—with the canni-
balistic, sacrificial rites of Barbara's family. One might feel relieved
that such savage practices, common enough in primitive cultures,
have been replaced by Christianity's more benign adaptations. Or
one may suspect that these drives are merely disguised by their
Christian shepherd's clothing and so permitted to live on.

Like Suzanna, Father Andrew has tended to see "these matters/more in the light of day . . ."; for him, though, "these matters" are markedly more personal and intimate. In his early speeches are several awkward, involuntary double entendres which lead to a revelation that in his teens Andrew had been molested by his favorite uncle. The surprising thing—to the reader as to himself—is that, despite this abuse (or because of it?) he continued to love his uncle. We, like Father Andrew, have seen in Barbara a deeply related linkage of violence to love and sex; worse, either factor may be causal. We suspect a crucial ambiguity in Barbara's description of her own ritual violation:

> . . . your father goes first,
> and calls you his best girl.
> You're so scared you love him
> in the center of your heart, . . .

Is she scared *that* she loves him or scared and *therefore* loves him? She later admits that "There's an ecstasy like sex/in the most horrible thing that can happen." Telling of her mother's near drownings of her own children, she reports:

> The only word I know to tell you
> what my mother's face looked like
> is *lust*, like all the power in the world
> wouldn't be enough to make her sure
> she was alive.

The earliest violation by her father involved a similar access of power:

> He likes the drops of blood,
> the breaking through what isn't
> his. It is some kind of ritual
> that makes everything belong
> to him.

This same linkage of sex and violence appears in her telling of her abduction by the man she later married:

> . . . I saw Joe standing there so mean
> he might have been my father, so of course
> I fell in love at once. I was so scared,

I had to make it with him right then. When I saw
he stuttered really bad, I knew he loved me
for the way I came at him, sure of myself,
and taught him tricks. Then he could
beat me up and even out the score.

I am reminded of a marvelous and terrifying statement by Simone
Weil:

"The powerful ones of this world, if they push oppression
beyond a certain point, inevitably make themselves adored." Weil
goes on to explain that when mistreated, we dare not see that those
with power over us may not care whether we live or die, may indeed
enjoy our sufferings; we interpret our persecution as an expression of
their love and concern. So with Barbara, who recognizes that her
sexual complaisance may cause Joe to love her, but will also make
him feel so weak and vulnerable that he'll need to abuse her to
reassert his power.

At this point, we should probably broach a question which
may arise for many readers. When some recent spectacular stories of
parental abuse and/or Satanism have proven to be confabulations—
inventions which the supposed victims have come to believe actually
occurred—what are we to think of Barbara? Obviously, one cannot
investigate the history of a fictional character as one might a real
person; if the poem gives no information about such a concern, I
suggest that it has no such concern. What matters is that this woman
has encountered, either in her mind or in the world around her, very
real horrors—things that have been done to someone, some time,
some place, things which still exist in our psyches and so might be
re-enacted. Even more, the poem is concerned with how her
revelations have brought others to reconsider their own lives.

All this may seem like very bad news—though we might
recall that bad news is often more needful, more useful than good.
Yet the prognosis for Barbara, who came to seek help, seems fairly
good. Her various selves may not be completely united; they *are*
talking to each other. Though memories of her childhood's attic
terrors keep her from going "upstairs" to take part in the church
service, she does stay downstairs, caring for the younger children. If
that might seem the worst news of all, Barbara appears kindly
enough in her attentions. And this has a certain symbolic right-
ness—our children are all raised by forces or by people haunted by

archaic terrors and ferocities. Barbara finds she can watch one of her young charges exploring her own body to "find the parts of herself"; she can manage to repair such small losses as her own loose tooth without "the old panic of falling apart."

I trust I've made it clear how highly I regard these poems. To take a character whom most would think either deranged or so deeply damaged as to be irreparable—in any case, so extreme as to deserve only that sensationalistic attention found in TV "magazines"—and instead to see her involvement with the broader range of humanity seems to me a splendid achievement. If it might lead one to despairs, it could also elicit hope. Of course we all come of bad stock; if not the devil's children, we are at least his nieces and nephews. Given our bad bloodlines, the fact that we have created a culture so fertile, so inventive and even (occasionally) merciful might induce, if not good cheer, at least admiration.

—W. D. Snodgrass

Contents

III
Exsultet on Holy Saturday

IV
Father McGuire's *New Baltimore Catechism*, Lesson 19

V
I sleep, but my heart waketh

Kyrie eleison

I.

Father McGuire's *New Baltimore Catechism*, Lesson 28

1. Rosalie, when preparing for her First Holy Communion, said to her mother: "Do you really mean that I will actually receive into my body—the body and blood, soul and divinity of Our Lord Himself?" Give the answer of this lesson to that question.

Barbara

If I tell you all of it,
you have to get ready.
Bad things happen in this world.
Some people just plain want to be bad,
like God's best angel Lucifer
who wouldn't do what God thought of,
but headed out like a mad dog
across the biggest difference
he could find. Some people would
kill you if they could, or break
your bones. You have to know
who they are, and where, and where
God is. Sometimes it's hard
to find out which is which.

Suzanna

Tell me all of it. I am already moving her words to safety.
I am writing, "She is shifting her bag arm to arm with the precision

of the blind." I have her eyes wide open as if she had just dragged me
out of a dream, or out of the snow, here to St. Anthony's hall.

I don't know what she thought, seeing me here off and on, that I
could pray for her, maybe, that I am not a pagan who only prays

to the thought of praying, coming here to see if my presence
will yet screw up the ancient organization of the universe.

What she has told me, these weeks, Good God, I keep moving away.
Someone is drinking coffee and talking now, trying to approximate

small talk. I am writing in my head, not just recording, but thinking of
a phrase, "the precision of the blind," getting not the thrill of strangeness

but of recognition, my own life exaggerated. My body, then, is part
of the completion of the scene, another specimen. Notice how

when people talk, they find an exact space between themselves.
The true exchange is memory touching, a spot sexual in its tenderness,

favored like a bad knee. We pray around it. It is the darkest corner
of a house we remember, the most primitive terror that does not reject us,

indeed, comes to find us, to tell us everything. She's fastened across
from me like Judgment Day. Two people, snow having a fit

against the windows, and now the plow will have to get us out.
I try to imagine the thirteen Eskimo words for snow. How many

points of view are possible? Who am I talking to? Sometimes I catch
the glint of different people, the way you see the parent in the child

by a turn of the chin, a laugh: shards of a story too big for one teller.
What's settled or unsettled in me is dangerous as a burglar.

Barbara

I started out my mother's
best child. I didn't cry.
She had my sister Marsha first,
at least first with my father, if
Marsha was his. Then me, while
my father fought overseas.
She gave me to Grandma, who spoke
only Polish, wore only black.
I didn't learn English
until I was two.
I didn't learn to crawl because
the old woman would smash my hands
with her black shoes.

I remember a dozen candles
along her bedroom walls, saints
on her mantle single-file.
She gets me ready to take up
Devil things, knowing for sure
I am really her son's child,
conceived under her own roof.
She bathes me and bathes me,
chanting that stupid Polish
from before I was born,
taking my ears and cleaning them
out, just like that.
She burns my feet
in the candles, but I know to go
to the light, not try
to run away, but go straight
into the flame and rise up
out of myself to the light. . .

There's a child so small
she has no name. She is very quiet,
so no one will know she's here.
There's another child. She watches
the first one suffer in the flame.
She stands in her crib.

She is not afraid because
she lives over here.
She is a different one. She chooses
any name she likes,
not Barbara, the name
they gave her first,
but the name of someone who might
be held and spoken English to.

When the father comes home
at last from the war, she watches
him take off the diaper and poke
into the silent one
with his finger.
He likes the drops of blood,
the breaking through what isn't
his. It is some kind of ritual
that makes everything belong
to him. I am high and still, unborn
in God's white arms. I am
holding my own blood far down inside
where everything is black.

Suzanna

I take off my glasses and bury my head in the steam
of the coffee, but it seems as if I am bending slow motion

over something else: the left foot of my friend Burdett Palmer,
thirty years ago. My mind is moving through steam rising off

the snow. Two boxcars stand misplaced in front of the station,
a crowd hushed around the shoe, beside the rails.

They say Burdett stepped between the couplings just as the links
pulled tight and sliced the bottom off his foot. Everything

waits for inspectors from Chicago. I am only seventeen,
so I have to stick my nose in the shoe, to see the private insides

of a foot, flecked with snow. My mind starts gathering as fast
as it can—doubling, quadrupling, cloning a whole body, pushing

the body out of myself, giving it a life, making it run down
the track with both fine feet, hell-bent for the meeting of the rails.

Barbara

A demon comes out of the attic
at night, but it is only my father
with his needles, guns, knives,
him and his army buddies, stopping
over for the weekend, without
their wives. Him and his buddies
and the rest. They drink
and pass the family album around,
its black tooled leather,
its photos of human arms and legs
and heads, loose pieces of strangers
among the pictures of us girls.
Our first communion pictures, then,
                                those.

You know what's going to happen
that night. You're lined up
in little robes. Geisha girls?
I used to think that's what we were.
I wanted some plain name for us.
First, they make you watch war movies
on TV so you can't be sure
what's real, the TV blood gets so
confused with what goes on upstairs.

Then you begin your delicate
process of turning away
into your other people, petals
of a flower: I am named Sarah,
the one who tells you this in a
whisper. I am invisible Martha.
You can never find me. I am Me,
who knows what to do
to get by. Me is not Barbara.
They're different. . .

                Then we have to
walk through black curtains
into hell. It's Me they tie up,
I think, next to my sister Marsha.

Someone, maybe it's Me,
has to watch them slice up
a black dog, its gulping yelp,
into a hundred pieces. Someone
will be next. Someone is tied
in the same way. Someone would die,
except that they go into her
with themselves, instead of knives,
over and over, all of them.

Father Andrew, up at St. Anthony's,
who listens to me all the time
now, he never says anything
about all this
that happened. He starts saying
what love is, but
how do you know, except to take
what you're given? It's all
you have, and your father goes first,
and calls you his best girl.
You're so scared you love him
in the center of your heart, where it
just starts to crack into petals.

Father Andrew

Three feet of snow
and still falling, Barbara shows up
to light a candle, keep our regular
appointment. Twice a week
she takes the bus all the way from Parma,
comes dressed in sweater and skirt
like it's Sunday, two gold crosses
to protect her neck.

                         Leave the past
behind, other priests have told her,
as if the ancient evils can walk
right in, if you let them, past
the service leaflets.

I wonder what the Bishop
would say. Exorcism? It's still done.
I've always seen these matters
more in the light of day, myself.
I sit with Barbara in the pew
in my white cassock I put on for her.
We watch invisible stirrings get caught
in rows of votive candles. Then
she wants me to stand at the altar,
span the distance between God
and her with my large body, the Church.
She watches my lips pull the name of God
out of thin air. I won't pretend I'm not
afraid, too. There's some snare
in this bringing forth, a backside
to worry about, and who
am I? Just Andy Hill. Sometimes
it's just me. I got stuck two times
in the snow. I'm lucky I'm here.

Barbara

In the first grade, I fell in love
with a nun whose arm wrapped
around my shoulders every day.
My father laughed at me.
I wanted to be a nun, but then
you get so confused you don't know who
the real God is. You pass through
those black curtains upstairs
as if you'd turned a biscuit over
and found it burnt on the bottom.
Everyone's murmuring, doing a
shuffle-walk. They're all in robes
and you can't see their hands
clamped on the space under the robes.
I get afraid of nuns in church
with their hands beneath the black. Who's
going to do us bad? Every night
I opened my heart to God
as quietly as a fern, not knowing
what to ask, except to catch
the rhythm of the night train passing.
I was so light I went away
with the train, and sleep would come.
If they came to get me
in the night, it wasn't me they got.

When they come to get me,
they eat me up like the Host at church,
all around me in a circle, biting
my flesh, no part untouched. They go
in my ears, my nose, making their noises
and chants, but they won't get fat
on me. I have been gone a long time
on the train. I don't know who's
here. I don't hate her,
I just don't know her name, or why
she's willing to take my place.

Father Andrew

Today I visit the children.
They see me coming, my blurry black
form through frosted glass.
Their plaid uniforms
and crayon drawings waver on
the other side. The nuns have arranged
everyone for my questions—
this year's class slated for
the first two sacraments, penance
and eucharist. Best students up front;
hopeless ones at the back.
In between, those useful as
a backdrop, or screen.

      "Your souls are
precarious," I tell them.
"The Devil will want you
more than ever. His temptations
are glamorous. Who can tell me
what the word temptation means?
Who can tell me
where the Devil lives?"

What must I seem to them,
a white-haired lumpy man holding
answers, my spotted hands
gathered to myself?
      "Miss Fox, What is the fourth
commandment?" A glaze of fear
near the back of the room.
Sister stares at the top of Miss Fox's
unwashed head, angry, expectant.
I wonder how love came down
to this. I print words
on the blackboard ten inches tall,
hoping to break letters
through to sense.

        All the same, most of us stop
at images. We're made of flesh.
It's a mystery to me
how some blessed children have it
in them to see through bulk
like mine, askew among the tiny desks.
Lord, I know I need to lose weight,
but it's so infernally hard,
all the sweet things
people bring, and the good bread
Sister Bernetta makes!

Barbara

Saturday is fast day. We're locked
outside all day, nothing
to eat. For a while, I dump pebbles
in a truck, then I want to sit
on the step, my face in my hands.
By evening, my stomach almost forgets
what makes it cramp.
Then Sunday, my father cooks
a feast—salad, chicken, the whole
thing! Nothing else matters.
At bedtime they give us paragoric,
measured so we can still stand up,
and the laxative.
They have it figured almost to the hour
what will go through the bowels.
First, what they do in the attic
is they get all their sperm in you,
and they tie you on a cross
that spins, and leave you upside
down to let Satan's sperm go down.
It's very holy. They tell you it's
coming all the way through,
out of your mouth. They say the words.
What they say is very important.
When they take away the blindfold,
there is my black father in front
of the light, pressing my stomach,
and that's when my bowels
let go. The words, and I am soaked
and cramping. What they have to do is
put words inside my private
self, where I don't talk. I am so
ashamed, so ashamed, cleaned out
with shame, then gone! I barely know
when they blow air up inside me,
a motor-thing blowing it in. It makes
a little hum, less than
a word. Nothing else
matters. What you have to do is say
one thing only, let everything else go.

Suzanna

I'm the oldest child, always digging around in things,
playing doctor: "Tell me, *when did the trouble start?*"

Just last Christmas, I asked my mother: How was I born?
That one point where we last met, although I keep trying.

She tells me nothing beyond the usual, except
that the anesthetic didn't work. She tells it as if she had long since

left that body and come to where she is,
away from everything. I feel around in my muscles

for what they remember, that register of pain closing up
in my center like a rose, her speechless muscles clamping down,

and Bingo, I have fallen off the edge of her,
unfolding and sleepy, the memory of her cry sheering away

from me, something to feel guilty for through
all the pleasures of life. The world needs more comfort

than I can give it. Barbara watches me write down her words,
the one who's supposed to shift their terrible burden.

I'm not Father Andrew. Might as well watch the snowplow
rasp the street to the quick and pull back, *ee ee, ee ee.*

Barbara

You want to know how easy
it is to lift a man from his daily
life and make him disappear
like a sucked-in breath? My father
and his friends cruise the streets
of Cleveland and load up some
old drunk who'd go anywhere
for another drink. They bring him
to our house and tie him up,
and me next to him. He's one kind
of sacrifice, I'm another. Just
before a man dies, he turns sober
as a judge, and I can tell you
fear has a smell that comes through
even alcohol. His face lolls
toward mine, his blonde hair.
They leave him nothing to see
with, or talk with. His face
empties like when you've forgotten
something you know you need.
They take off everything
he can live without.
My father pulls the black hood up.
He raises the knife
over his head. There's a fine line,
like a horizon, that passes through
me. Do you feel it passing
through you? Some things you can't
know. I turn away, indifferent
as a whore when they turn
to me. They'll cut him up,
and even put his teeth in separate
graves. No police will come.
Father Andrew won't hold up his hands
the way he does with me, and call
the parts of that old man's
life together again.

Suzanna

I don't know if evil is absence or presence.
Our father used to sneak up the stairs, creak,

creak. Abby and I giggling under the covers.
"It's the Grammash!" he'd growl, step by step,

and pounce on the covers with a horrible roar
we tried to believe in, almost falling

over into tears, as if we had made up something
too big to keep out, with our little hands.

Barbara

I'm not making any of this up,
although it's taken all these years
to get my selves talking to each other.
You have to save yourself by tucking
little parts away in so many different
places, no one can find them all.
I've kept my soul, for instance,
in my wrist all this time. It's very white
and miles from the blood
of the heart, or the other blood,
and who would think to look there?
It barely flutters at all, as if
a baby just started kicking.

I'm 41. I have three kids: Angel,
Joe, and Vito. Angel has two children
now. She's delicate. Her second child's
been sick. I've been afraid, it seems
like I might have passed on
downhill thoughts, you know. But
Little Joe's in love,
and Vito goes to school, at least,
and hangs around the house the way
fifteen-year-olds do, drifting through
the last of being a kid.
It's a miracle they call my house home.
It makes me think the world
is anxious to be good. Like if you
put down a sidewalk, in a few years,
the grass will burn through
the hardness like green flames. Last year
I graduated high school,
learned to type, which means
I don't have to work on the line,
standing on my feet all day.
Joe sends his checks mostly on time,
and I changed my number, so he
can't call and confuse me anymore.

II.

Father McGuire's *New Baltimore Catechism*, Lesson 27

1. While you are at Mass, why ought you to feel the same as if you were at Christ's crucifixion on Good Friday?

Father Andrew

I demonstrate to the children
how the Cardinal will slap
their cheeks, make them soldiers
in the church militant, marked
forever, no annulment—

I open my low vowels
on suffering, how one will suffer
for the Church, outcast in this world.
Hands folded, row behind row,
scallops of arms and hands, they are
waves breaking
toward a black tower, which is
me, augmented, vested. They are casting
toward me, wanting to reach
the finish, far from
the slow, dangerous bottom, over which
I am myself swimming, only child,
going on fourteen, counting strokes
in Lake Michigan before breakfast,
my favorite time! With the light
barely up, I can still balance
my mother, my father, and God.
I am stinging like a soldier with it,
the saving and pushing away.

Down these rows of desks I call
each Christian name, ask a question,
watch their cheeks blanch,
wanting and not wanting a chance.

Barbara

We practice saying the words
in the leather book:
Deception. Destruction. Despair.
Over and over.
They line us up, tallest to smallest,
and I'm so near the end
I might fall off.
Uncle George, Aunt Toby, Uncle Paul, John,
barely faces under the hoods.
Martha told me who they were.
I didn't want to see my family there,
but she just had to say their names
because she used to be so small
she couldn't say anything.
Now the people here inside me
are all talking to each other—
I can't explain how it happened.
Sometimes I get scared
the way we're letting each other in
like grownups at the door.
Barbara's the name of the open space
we go in and out of. Whew!
What does Barbara mean? As if any
names are big enough to fill her up.

Suzanna

I would like to say *Barbara* and have her look up, exact and clarified.
Later, we watch the ducks on the edge of the pond, just off the ice.

She's afraid, the way the ducks flare unpredictably, whole families
of hope, chasing us. I pick up a silver feather, a knife of a feather,

my efficient gesture of cleaning the landscape. I shoo the ducks,
nothing left but us. So, we're walking, dirty footprints in the snow—

the word dirty, as if white's the answer. To get, say, a million dark
faces firmly baptised into light. When I was nine, Dr.

Clarence E. Lemon lowered me into the water, white handkerchief
over my nose. Great-aunt Nell gave me a Bible—white leather,

with Suzanna Marie Ross in gold, pressed into the prophets and saints
forever. I was washed in the blood of the Lamb, my lace dress

with the ribbons soaked, cloth against flesh and bones, and under
my bones, inside the marrow of the bones, I was dead,

dead to sin. Who are you, then, when you die? At this moment,
I am trying to hear Barbara's voice coming up under mine, mouth

of my mouth, seeking me out, scared half to death. And naming names,
each gravitating to the other like atoms, making the world appear.

Barbara

I named myself Sarah, out of the Bible.
That's Abraham's wife. Would she
have let him lower the knife on Isaac
even if God said so? But who was she
to say no? Shhh. You barely
have to move your lips to make my name
come out. I know a lot more things
than I can tell. Maybe I've stood
beside the knife:
the worst secret is myself. Maybe
I'm one of their children
who won't get bigger.
Am I bigger than I think?
My father gets big when he puts the horns
on his forehead. He wears his teeth,
for the biting. Other times
he leaves them small and swimming
in a glass. My sisters and I chase
each other with them, clattering
to make ourselves bigger.

Father Andrew

"Welcome, little sister, little
brother," the Cardinal will say,
anointing the foreheads
of the children with chrism,
like a balm, not for his little slap,
but for the deep ache....

There is this
the children can yearn for—
to be beautifully alone,
suffering. God the most secret
of lovers. Then the world
seems not so much
to give up, in return.

What have I given up? One girl.
Julia. Whose molasses hair poured
over from her desk to mine,
whose turning around to me one day
I remember as a slow Be-Bop, an ache
of bass drums

still in my hips. Arthritis in
the ball-and-socket joint, so deep
I can't get to it with BenGay.
Makes me wince against the edge
of the teacher's desk.

Barbara

You want to be your parents' best girl—
you go to school, you listen to the nuns,
you confess your sins. Is it a sin,
what wraps around your heart and breaks
your breath in two? You never tell this.
The world seems like your own
body, your head caught
in the sun, your bowels raging
underneath. You learn in science class
a cell divides at the waist, each
half making up its own complete thought.
You wonder if cells feel like halves
or whole....
                    My sunshine name
is Patty. She's sure her mother
and father love her very much.
She likes the word *abiding. Faith*
abiding. The hope of things unseen.
Saturday night, her aunt Toby curls her hair
with rags. For Sunday, Patty has learned
to say the three ways guardian
angels help us: *by praying*
for us, by acting as messengers from God
for us, and by serving as our guardian
angels. Angels have no bodies, so
they fasten their smiles on the stars,
to keep them shaped like smiles.
Angels wear yellow and white dresses,
so you can see where they are, but
if anyone tries to tie them
to a table, they can take off
their dresses and have no waists at all.
They get as hard to hold onto
as singing, abiding all over the universe.

Suzanna

You want to be their best girl, get things down
right. The eternal never sleeps, getting things right:

Aristotle went to sleep every night with his arms
outstretched, holding a bronze sphere in his hand,

holding it over a pan. A moment's giving way
and the ball would clatter in the pan!

I could've stayed awake better, gotten Barbara down
better, the way her footbones align and shift

on the snow. Picture her walking away from me,
a small woman, delicate steps. Vertical symmetry.

It's built into our genes to pay attention to
vertical symmetry. It might be another creature,

also human, all the hopes and dangers of that.
In the beginning, the dividing line between self

and other was no more than a membrane of lipids,
sugars, proteins. Then pseudopods, to embrace

the edible; flagella, to run away—a grab bag of tricks,
perfectly in motion, hungering, just hungering,

nothing fancy....

Barbara

Afternoons when my father went out,
my mother liked to fill the bathtub
with scalding water and put us
in it. She told us once
her father almost drowned
when she was young, and I wondered if
she thought something remained
to be done. I'm looking up through
water at my mother's face.
To this day
her face is water to me.

One Monday she took my baby sister
Diane into the bathroom.
Diane was my father's pet,
and mother hated her! I could hear
the water running behind the door.
I think it was Sarah, then,
making my lips get ready
for NO, but only a rush of air
came out, like a tire going down.
My skin and bones got huge and hollow.
Who could find a way
out of that cave, to rescue anyone?

At last my mother came out
holding the gasping child, her
spindly legs dangling from the towel.
The only word I know to tell you
what my mother's face looked like
is *lust*, like all the power in the world
wouldn't be enough to make her sure
she was alive. She took up the whole
living room, and I had to stand
inside her like a couch, or chair.

Father Andrew

I re-route my lusts—fast
once a month, try to stand firm
against minor parochial dangers.
But sometimes I am an old mammal.
I lurch out from beneath
myself, predatory,
stiff with misery.

I try to understand this.
Everything's forgiveable, when
you know what causes what.
But when the lurching comes,
it seems larger than a moment's
thought, a match

for prayer. Lizards rise
out of sewers, angels come
like fields of butterflies.
Thousands of angels lighting on
the backs of lizards! What if
neither knows the other is there?

Barbara

My first communion, the nuns
gave me a white Bible and a rosary.
All the way home, I touched them
and touched them as if I could
work my way inside with my fingertips.
Well, of course when I got home,
they took them from me
and tied me up, my head turned
so I'd have to watch them circle up
and pee on them like a fountain
at the mall. I decided if I could
keep the Bible in my eyes,
I'd be OK. But they moved it
out of sight. They were cutting up
puppies. It's my communion:
they make me eat the chunks
of meat. My head hurts so bad
the pain turns into nothing at all.
When it's everywhere, you give up,
and what you once called pain,
you start to call yourself.
They're putting things inside
every place I've got—putting in
the rosary, the chunks of meat.
"See who has the most power?"
they tell me. "The priest can only
put the Host inside, but we can
take it out again." I see it's true.
I am truly the Devil's child,
puppy's tails coming out, oh,
coming out of me, and only
this morning I swallowed God.
The Devil must need God, I think,
to show him what the best things are,
so he'll know what to hurt the most.

Father Andrew

Almost, I am reconciled
to this open altar, parishioners
circled in the ancient way,
like a mob, tongues out. I used to
give them the translucent
disk that melts like snow,
unleavened for the old pain
of slaughter, the judgment
of the Lord upon Egypt.
Now I do like risen
bread, the way it tears
apart, the substantial feel
of it in the mouth.
Remember the hearts
of the Israelites, I say,
quickened to cross the desert.
They made even the promised land
out of rich food—
milk and honey!
I teach the children: think of
Jesus on the cross, Jesus rising
again. It's like the wheat
ground down, the dough,
the firing. *Don't be afraid*
to live, to know what comes
next. That's what I want to say.
Nothing but bread
will break the boundary
between itself and you. Nothing
but bread, to make
bright eyes, radiant cheeks.

Barbara

In the sixth grade I started
growing a child inside me. Later
I knew, but then I didn't know
what made anything happen,
they put so many things in so many
different places. How I found out
is they tied me down
and rammed and rammed me
until the child turned loose
and bled right out of me. They got
so excited! They caught
it in a silver cup—
a little heart, deep and red.
When they made me drink it,
it slid down like a raw egg, oh God,
I know how hard it is for you
to hear what I have to say.
Martha knew it then.
She kept the secret for me
like a silver locket you don't
pass on until your child's
old enough to treat it right. Then
you know it's out of your hands.
A few months ago,
Martha told Sarah, who whispered it
to me so low I could hardly hear,
but the delicate bones in my ear
knew what she had to tell.
They started this tremor
that spread and spread until it
came out of me like a red-hot
bowling ball, like a baby
when it crowns and spreads
your hips until it's the end
of the world, but another
world's coming, another's coming,
if you can give just one more push.
... And what you hold afterward
makes you live and die more
than you ever thought possible.

Suzanna

Evil and suffering are not the same thing.
I have not believed in evil. This happened, that

resulted. My sister and I used to sit
cross-legged on our twin beds, working it out:

Mama Gwynn, Grandpa Larry, Aunt Nell, the exact
location of first wounds, their logical route

to Apple Road, where at the moment they lived,
raging through the bedroom wall from our parents'

side. If anything broke, no one was to blame, no
pain, just the reported facts of disaster. Look me

flat in the eye, little sister, here we go,
nerve pathways switching up to the breathless

cortex. We are thinking, Abby, therefore we
are. We can see everything from here, the huge and

classic movie of the world, only a few loose
sparks shooting straight from *thalmus* to *amygdala*:

you can have those words. Put them in your
mouth, make them work for you, climb them up

through the sound track. I can draw you a picture of
how it works, the refinement of the new brain above

the old, good and evil no more admissible in this
science than sobs, their shameful raggedness.

Barbara

I know my name is Mike
as soon as I wake up in the garage,
tied down under a single bulb,
somebody's face between, somebody's
tattoed arms. Somebody has to get mad,
and I am the one, the only one
with muscles hard enough.
Forceps, needles, scalpel,
squint up from the table.
Then they reach inside me
to cut my penis off.
I'm fourteen. I always thought
if I could grow up a little more,
my penis would be outside,
but it must be still inside,
which is why they hate me
enough to want to cut it out.

I always wanted a baby
the size of my thumb:
what they take out of me
with surgical gloves is small
as Poppy in my storybook. Then
they put me on the living room floor
looking up at the end tables,
flowered slipcovers, gossip bench,
an army my father's lined up
to watch me hurt. They tell me
a banana made me sick!
Something's tied across my mouth,
but I am not there, anyway.
I am crouched down here
in the hollow between my legs,
soaking up rage at what they took
away. The more I feel the walls
of me empty, the more I storm,
but very quietly like a black eye
turning purple, then yellow,
then nothing much else to see.

Father Andrew

Andrew the fisherman, brother
of James—I imagine his heart
raging in the heat, little heart
caught in the throng gathering
like a county fair
on the banks of the Jordan.
Everyone's hungry. He's sure
his walking away from the old,
ordinary nets was a terrible
mistake! Now he's in this,
this dubious truth, dragging him
all over the countryside.
And what will the people eat?

I fold my hands on the little
enamel table, try to tell
Sister Bernetta some of what
I know. She is pounding out
dough, for Danishes, I hope,
with little dollops
of raspberry jam in the center.
She turns away toward the sink,
I know she is crying.
Where are my tears? Nothing's
ordinary anymore. I put on
my coat, go out for a walk,
stop a long time in front of
Father Bruno's, Father
Willard's statues, taller
than life above the boxwoods.
Their eyes are made of holes
in the concrete. I am standing
in the driveway, casting in all
directions. That is why
I spread my arms, I am fishing
for comfort, so I can cry.

III.

Exsultet on Holy Saturday

O felix culpa, quae talem ac tantum meruit habere Redemptorem.
[O happy fault, which has deserved to have such and so mighty a
Redeemer.]

Barbara

Sometimes it makes me mad
that you don't know—underneath, any of us
might do anything. For instance,
we were children lined up to watch
the dogs bark at a naked baby in a cage.
Hungry dogs. You'll do anything not to be
that child. Yet, there's an ecstasy like sex
in the most horrible thing that can happen.

That's what happens. They lay you out
and suck and blow all the old you
out through your open places.
Your father licks you in secret patterns.
They clean your body out and lock you
in a black cage. Three days no food,
no water, you can't control
your bowels. You can't move.
If I move my finger, I'm not dead.
They talk to you, what you need to do
to get out. Does God rescue people
by letting them do what they have to do
to get out? So I'm raised, cleaned off.

I am high and powerful, walking
to the altar. I get to wear white.
I get to walk beside my father,
rosary beads around the top of my head.
My knife is double-edged, shiny buttons
on the handle. I say the words
over the child, a girl child, shove in
the knife. The patterns of my father's
tongue have taught me where to cut.
All my life is here, and everyone cheers
silently, their bodies like electric lights.

Suzanna

I resign from poetry, forever. I resign from dissecting
the evidence. I resign from leaning over the child close enough

to see its veins, from making the wince of blade-flash,
the terrible, barely human chants, like crows in the distance.

At this moment, hungry black crows are yelling and swooping
through our yard. My husband is nailing up the birdhouse

with SEE ROCK CITY painted on the side, while I have been
trying to interject these lines between me and evil.

What happens if a body is cut to pieces? Crows! We put up a feeder
with tiny holes, for chickadees only. I am overcome with

a sense of wrongdoing, of what I have rejected. Burdett Palmer's
foot lay open to me, sopped in blood. I flexed the little poem

of my own foot, its amazing, immortal veins. And here I am
still at it, poetizing as if I had never sworn off, steering through a

half-blind tunnel of words. There's still the Grammash,
I'm pretty sure, on his way up the stairs with his horrible roar.

Barbara

We arranged her bones
in a steeple. I remember thinking
the ultimate thing would be
to get cut like that, to die
at the highest point of giving up.
The saints did that. . . I wonder
if the saints looked down once
and saw how deep hell is,
and that's what made them take
the other route as far as it would go
on earth, and then let go, let hope
open out into something else.

Father Andrew

Hush. That's what I think. But
it is as if I just now shuddered awake
myself, while my drunken uncle is shoving his
penis into my face. How old am I? Too young
to know the name of what he's up to.
One can't escape. One steps off the edges
of one's flesh, into someone
else's. Sin breaks open
somewhere upstream. I can't do anything
about it, I am sick of it, yet it is
exceedingly, in thought, word,
and deed, through my fault,
through my fault,
through my
most grevious fault.

. . . that fault, and worse—children
falling on their bellies in death-camp
showers. Children crying, the high-
pitched ringing in my ears like a faulty
shower-head, showers of radiation
in the desert, showers
of gunfire in Colombia, Bosnia . . .

                    My uncle kept me
all afternoon, lying in uncut grass,
sun and shade swimming across
our bodies. Who could know?

I've been telling it in code.
I've grown up to be a stunt man, reenacting
scene after scene under lights: the fall,
the getting up again, wiping
the shame off my face, running home
to supper *hail Marys* all
the way. The details of the
dinner table, knives, forks,
checkered napkins folded into sails.

Barbara

My father made me get my teeth
pulled out
like his: this smile's
not mine. I finally had my womb
cut out, too, so he couldn't
fill it any more.
What parts can I cut out
of my life to make it clean?
I go to church, now,
and I am afraid.
Last week I stayed to pray.
An old man saw my tears
and smiled at me
when I got up,
his innocence coming toward me
like a tiny boat headed for a waterfall.
Forgive yourself,
Father Andrew says.
He puts his hand
on my head
and I am one
of those children
in the picture with Jesus
with the lambs and flowers,
but when I walk out
the church door
to the bus stop, I am
as big as I get, almost
monstrous, little people
edging around me.

Suzanna

Sometimes I don't want a church. I don't like God to wait
in the gloom, God like a father bent over his boat frames

down in the garage, molding them one by one in a vise.
I am very small, watching. I can see the luminous unclaimed

field of my body. Here he comes, each one of the stairs
bending! I remember a good plot to keep God occupied:

Once upon a time a man got mixed up in a machine with a fly,
came out a giant, raging fly with a suffering human heart,

heart and fly at war for his girlfriend. "Let me die of this,"
he begs at last, lying in a pool of his own spit. She,

in a mixture of revulsion and ecstasy, kills him at the end.
I hear a small child weeping, she believes the movie

is true. Sometimes I have to tell myself it's frames on a reel.
Picasso knew what's real, what's not, what the real eye sees,

how it jerks imperceptibly from angle to angle like a fly's
eye, before the brain forgives everything and puts it all together.

Barbara

This is how all these years I kept going
in the same direction: Saturday night
my friend Marilyn and I were fooling around
the shopping center when Joe and his friends
threw me in the trunk of his car
and drove out of town. They opened the trunk
in the middle of a pitch black field
and I saw Joe standing there so mean
he might have been my father, so of course
I fell in love at once. I was so scared,
I had to make it with him right then. When I saw
he stuttered really bad, I knew he loved me
for the way I came at him, sure of myself,
and taught him tricks. Then he could
beat me up and even out the score.
This time when I got pregnant, I didn't know
if it was my father's or Joe's, but it was
something I wanted to wrap around tight.
The night I married Joe, my mother threw me out,
my father sat in his chair, mouth closed.
Two weeks later Joe's uncles and cousins
sat down at my kitchen table and told me,
"If Joe wants to beat you up, that's OK.
If he wants to cheat on you, that's OK."
Then they left. And my father kept coming over,
making me be his wife, too. I felt like
I lived in the trunk of a car.
When Angel was born I locked myself
in the bathroom, away from her crying.
She was so small when she cried, her veins
showed like little maps, and I didn't want to
take her anywhere I had ever been before.

Father Andrew

I used to come in from school—
living room dim as a cave,
four toddlers napping on their rugs,
and three cribs to step around
to the kitchen, maybe help my mother
fold half a dozen diapers,
making ends meet, before one child
after the other would open
its eyes, rub its sticky nose
across its face. One cry
after the other, tuning up.
I see this from arched windows,
stones vaulting like the upper chambers
of the brain. Behind me,
the quire lines up like vocal cords;
in front of me the transept-dome
gathers all of us into its
whale-belly.
                      What I believe in is
fractal geometry. I read
about this in Popular Science—
A small inlet makes the same shape
as the whole coastline.
The smallest grains of things
double and triple, ad infinitum,
unfolding into huge maps
of themselves, deciding all the time,
like white blood cells,
whether to be guilty
or innocent. Suppose I pinched
the arm of one child, for meanness.
Suppose someone squeezed on me.
The bruise is a point of departure,
a longing, that chooses
mate after mate, unsatisfied—
until what? Someone says That's Enough
Here comes my mother, she says it.

Barbara

Queen Bee, my father called Angel.
He kept coming over, Joe was gone
so much. I had to, then, I had to do it
to my own child, what my father had done
to me. I had to make her bleed inside
to keep him from making her his.
This had to be done precisely
in the center of the world:
North South East West
Who loves you the very best?
Then I took her to the doctor three times.
Hysterical mother is what
the doctor called me, and I was.
Every time my father walked in the door,
I was his, will-less as the last dried apple
of fall. I cut up my little dog
in the kitchen, so I wouldn't cut up Angel
any more, and so I'd be my father's
little girl, the one he gave the hardest
pain, then touched with one soft finger
spreading out like ripples on a pond
to rock the pain to sleep.
Oh, Angel, little Joe, Vito,
I wake up in the middle of your lives
like a princess in a fairy tale,
my eyes able to see, but my body
grown over with vines. Any wicked
witch could have taken you in
while I lay dreaming my crazy dreams!

Suzanna

At the end of suffering—well, just before the end of it—
I see there is a door. Everyone's sick and tired of wars, of rapes,

of people cutting up other people on the multiple TV screens
of the twentieth century—but the door, I swear, seems like the last

thing. The crows are screaming "Wake! Wake!"
from the attic where no one has broken the cobwebs for centuries.

The hollow-eyed lizard-shape in the corner has been planning
for years exactly how to gnaw through the tenderest part

of your cerebral cortex. You must not open the door
until you have forseen this. Believe me, I am saying this to myself.

I'm saying, *don't let the smell of coffee, the sun at last*
spreading across the deck, distract you. I'm keeping my mind on

one thing—on pushing the thought of sun, all the amassed sun
striking the snow, into this waking up, what I feel sure, now,

I remember as the original passage into life,
blood and water mingled, all directions accounted for at last.

IV.

Father McGuire's *New Baltimore Catechism*, Lesson 19

4. Mary Ann says that it is wrong to keep looking at a bad motion picture or a bad book or paper, or anything else that is impure or immodest. What does this lesson teach us that shows she is right?

Barbara

Yashick is the mortician
who keeps the blood when
one of our people dies.
We also need a piece of hair
and particular bones, to bring
the person back. A fire is burning.
We raise huge bowls of blood
to the fire, to the prayers.
The life that's gone
begins to press into us.
We dip our hands in blood
and rub it on each other
so that the spirit of the dead one
can spread open our smallest cells
and climb in, the way a wolf
returns to its lair, settles down....

My father says to me
the day before he dies, "I should've
went into an old sailor's home."
            "No, Daddy, no," I tell him.
Then he kisses me goodbye,
sticks his tongue in my mouth.
            "Take care of my best daughter,"
he tells Joe, knowing the way
he beat me up, giving me to Joe.
When he's dead, I keep asking,
"Did you leave the ring on him?"
That ring feels like the hard core
of him, and I need to know
where it is. He had a finger missing,
from the war. All I can see is
the finger-gap, and the ring.

I think we try to bring him back.
I think we kill someone
to bring him back,
to use the blood and bones:
He doesn't come. He stays barely
out of reach, trying to tell me

what to do to take his place.
His spirit settles on me
like a growl from the back
of a cave. I don't have to go
in the cave, but I know
what lives there, the shape
of his mouth, and his hands.

Father Andrew

When my uncle's coffin had been removed
from the room, the uselessness of some parts
of the human body rose to my mind. For instance,
why do men have nipples? I was by then
fifteen, my own body becoming a displaced center
of gravity. I figured I could stay tough
and pliable as a scar through it all. But
my uncle, carefully fit in the box with his
wax hands crossed at the third button
of his clean shirt, seemed like a folktale meant
to frighten me. When they left with him, I
came out with a long, improbable
utterance, a sob. I told him I loved him.
I think it was the uselessness I loved, whatever
wouldn't fit the formula, so came out bent
in him, baroque and bad. The room was empty
enough by then to feel safe, so I could scare
up this little trouble, which I have since
had to be saved from, over and over.

Barbara

I drop my head into the well
of faces and pull up any one.
I am a snake, a trick of the body
at every corner. Last night I lay in bed
and out of my mouth, the rumble
of the animal that curls
in the center of my bones,
and my bones began a dance of their own.
It felt like what I was before
the first human on earth.
Then my teeth curved around
their own words before there were words.
Didn't the whole human race kill
to get into its peaceful towns,
all its plowed fields?
Far down in me the dark stranger
refuses everything, breaks
every thought against himself,
his whole shape made up of what he breaks.

       I raise my head, I come up
Bobby, unjustly accused! I did
what I had to do, to survive.
Barbara bought that split-level place
on Harmony Lane, so how could she
pay for it? I take over the case,
as usual, straightening out finances.
The others get out of the way,
shadows clearing up.
I don't even like them, lolling around
in her skin, waiting for the world's
grievances to come in.
I bleach my hair raunchy, metallic.
I stand beautiful as a god
between Barbara and the snaky dark.
I walk beside my father, head up,
the dark stranger almost hidden
in my shadow. I am exactly the right
size and shape, like an eclipse.

Suzanna

If you wanted to get Adam and Eve out of the mindless
garden, I guess you'd think up a snake. The snake would be

barely a thin route out, nothing to worry about, per se,
a way to get them hiking across the exposed skin

of the planet. Cain's another matter, though, scary as hell,
totally out of control. I don't know what to do with him,

agent of nothing but his own blind self, the black hole
of himself that sees nothing else as real. A father could be

on his way up the stairs, his body with its black whorls of hair.
Everything else could feel like rubbery dream legs,

going nowhere. A mother could curl so deep in her recliner,
she's one dot, then lost in a universe of naugahide.

There could be a small child up there, going hazy. She stands
closing down her eyes, her ears, her heart. Oh, she keeps

a threadlike opening that works like a tin can telephone.
Someone still might speak through it and vibrate her heart.

Barbara

Lately, Marcie wants to go back
to Joe. I helped her pack.
We went, but I made her come home.
I know her.... It's Marcie
went to bed with Joe all
those years. She's the one
her father took to the air base
when she was fifteen. Anybody
can touch her who wants to,
anybody will do. She climbs
naked on the oil drums,
dances whatever she makes up
to put her body in their faces,
dances while the men clap
and sing. Her breasts shake
and she's proud. She smiles
and bends over, star
of the movies they make,
spreading her cheeks, turning
herself inside out, pulling
things out, putting things in,
making it all the same, outside
and in, so there's no Marcie
left to burn. There's no Marcie,
but her father works the furnaces
at the air base. After hours,
he shoves bodies inside,
the leftover pieces he brings
from home. They come out
like lumps of coal. I see it
like a TV show. I turn off the show.
I keep turning off the show.

V.

I sleep, but my heart waketh; it is the voice of my beloved that knocketh, saying, Open to me, my sister, my love, my dove, my undefiled: for my head is filled with dew, and my locks with the drops of the night.

Song of Songs

Barbara

After my father died, one night
I went up to bed. Was I asleep
or what? I saw this glow,
this light. For years after,
I thought it was
my father. The only thing
the light said was "Everything
will be OK now." I don't
think it was my father at all.
I think it was God, but I'm
so afraid of Him. I thought I
had Him tucked so far inside, then
He got out, by Himself.

Father Andrew

My father sat in my dark room,
holding his hands together.
It looked like prayer but felt
like he was traveling away
so fast I was cast up
on my twin bed in the wake
of his despair. I put my palms
together, thinking I
could follow. *Dear God*: letting
that stand for the one time
my father took me to Arnold's
bait shop, squeezed me
against the tub to let me pick out
bloodworms by myself. "That's
twelve, my son can count
to twelve," he bragged
to the other men. "So give him
a baker's dozen, he'll outfish
me." *Dear God, the same luck,
please,* I prayed. *Let my father
catch anything he needs.*

Dear God: letting that stand
for the rage for living on.
My uncle's hand squeezes me.
Barbara squeezes her trouble against
me. Sometimes I can hardly breathe.
I puff up the rectory stairs
to my blue chair and my small TV
in the corner! I just sit down
and say *Dear God.*
What else can I do?
It gives me something to cast out
into, fills my lungs with air.
And sometimes the Holy Ghost
just seems to spread
my bronchioles. I am sitting
on the counter at Arnold's,
entertaining the small crowd,
dangling the eight-inch bloodworm,
making my father laugh.

Barbara

It's not exactly a crowd
in me, but more like one person
who's died over and over.
When each one's come, somebody's
had to die.

So when they let me watch Vito
born out of me, all bloody
in the mirrors, I couldn't raise
my head for weeks—terrible explosions
the doctor couldn't cure. He sent me
to a shrink, and I started shooting off
my mouth about Joe. The shrink said,
"Why do you hate your mother
and father so much?"

The next thing, I was crawling around
my kitchen floor, crying "Mamma,
Mamma!" Then it was Martha, I think,
curled in the fireplace when my mother
and father came in. Joe sent for them.

Ten days in the hospital. In group therapy,
women said "This is my seventh time in,
or my eighth." Well, I already knew
how to die, so I didn't need to stay.
And every day, Joe called.
        "You're not at home where you're
supposed to be," he'd say. "I'm going to
get a girl to take your place."
So I went home

to Joe. He followed me around all day.
If I made the bed, he'd unmake it.
If I started vacuuming, he'd unplug
the cord. If I heated water for tea,
he'd pour it down the drain. Then
the kids would come home from school,
and Patty would be there, all
smiles, so close to death.

Suzanna

Seems like opposite poles—clown face/death face, but
look at them, both white as sheets of paper—ready for anything!

As if white were blank, and not, as it is, all the colors of the
                                                    spectrum
reflected at once. Full and empty at the same time, you might say.

I'm thinking of Gregory Peck as Ahab on the Pequod's final deck,
eyeing his truth beyond all truths, a phantom whitening

on the horizon. The touching formality Peck got into his longing,
rejecting the world around him, projecting himself into the void,

Nada, Nicht, the Divine Emptiness, never suspecting he was part
of the truth himself, soon to be roped to it, peg-legged,

bushy browed, looking nothing like divinity. What could I
ever write to be transparent, to look through to this evil, this good,

and let them grind against each other without my manipulations?
Let them wear down to just seeing, hearing, speaking,

and the rest, and what these mean, taken separately,
and put together again, about the way the universe thinks?

Father Andrew

                    "My son Andy,"
my mother would say to the ladies
in Kresge's Department Store.
"He wants to be a priest,"
her face so bright it seemed as if

Jacob's ladder had come down
to me out of a night sky.
It was the 1950s. My uncle rubbed
like a black stone in my stomach,
my father cried in the dark,
my mother sang sad bits of songs
at the kitchen sink, loneliness
slipping like soapsuds across
her hands.

I put one foot, so to speak,
on the ladder's bottom rung, torn
between hopes. I looked
back. My mother whispered
to the phone, lips
grazing the black.

                    This: a lover:
a serpent in the telephone cord,
because I could not take care of her
well enough. My own mother!
Maybe I wanted to know nothing
more. Maybe I wanted to be an angel,
up and down the ladder between heaven
and earth, messages in my teeth. Who knows?
I climbed into the stars.
I would return, one priestly star
among stars, hushing
the sinful earth like snow.

Yes, well, I gained fifty pounds,
a big star! Here it is, the longing
I have learned to taste, to hear
in my belly. It's only me.

This is the plain truth,
I guess. Listen Devil, there are
limits to everything. See
these hands? Ten fingers,
chewed nails, rough cuticles,
all full of blessing.

Barbara

God sang me a message
on the radio on my way to work:
"Harden My Heart." But I wasn't
the one who hardened my heart
and walked away from Joe.
I think it was Mike, showing off
his muscles. Joe told the boys
to beg me to come home.
"Ma, I can't stand it,"
Vito said over the phone.
Joe got a travel agent to call
and say I'd won a trip to Hawaii,
with my husband. But I hardened
my heart. Then one night
he pulled up beside me
in the driveway
and held a pistol to my head,
so I went back, for a while....

In a dream I was passing
through room after room,
carrying my grandson Jason.
The rooms seemed like
bathrooms, with mirrors
drinking him up, and nothing
to stop him from the tub
drain, the lavatory drain.
Where could I put him,
to live? Then I woke up.

A place under my ribs
turned, like a compass,
and before I knew it, one day
I was moving toward light:

Angel puts Jason in bed with me
when she stays over.
Last night while he was asleep,
I kissed his little mouth,

sleeping in an O, and lay awake
for hours, so soft and light
I could never take hold of anything,
just watch Jason breathe, every
breath turning at the edge of a cliff.

Suzanna

It could be God on the radio. It would need to be a voice
to believe in, a Walter Cronkite voice from mid-America

where there's no accent at all, where people talk about
the weather, starting their day by consulting the inevitable.

The voice of God would sound so neutral it would be
almost inaudible. It would enter the left ear and lay a grid

of amazement over the particulars the right ear has already
labeled and arranged. The grid would fall as lightly as a

spider's web. It would probably seem like a dream.
In a dream, Barbara's wrapped in a flowered quilt, a mother

delicately strokes her hair. The ragged clothes of her sadness
are flung on the floor. Darkness climbs to the window

like suppertime, empty of nightmares. The thing about
this dream is how empty it is. Even when I wake up, it's that

simple, yawning, trying to remember what day it is. I don't know
why this would happen, or how. I have gotten to the part

where I would need to boldly enter the interior
world of the radio where the little people are singing.

Barbara

I still won't go upstairs
where they drink the wine
and Father Andrew's words make
one plain hour scary. I sit
very still in the nursery rocking chair,
holding someone else's child
during church—you don't know
what it means, the child asleep
on my uncertain lap, with the place
under my breasts noisy as that photo
of Vietnamese children running
naked down a fiery dirt road.

So much gets buried....
Probably I remember how I would
touch my sister's hair, falling
asleep, and say, "We're twins,"
or "Sleep back-to-back all night."
What I want God to be is one
half-asleep touch, light as snow,
drawn up in itself because it loves
itself. Upstairs, the bell: the cup's
being raised, or the bread
split apart.

In the first crib is Kirsten, then
Kelly, then Allen, then Robert,
and I'm holding Bethann. I watch her
wake and find the parts of herself,
her hands and feet dancing in front
of her face like toys....

The bell makes the most awful longing,
and the longing brings the lost
bodies of strangers home
to me, when, certainly, I don't
want them, but I let them in,
and rock, hushing them down,
the chair crying out in its thin
wood that sounds like a song,

and maybe it is, maybe it is.
Anyway, it makes you happy enough
to stay down here, instead of
having the whole thing, upstairs.

Suzanna

Father Andrew's kissing the cup on the mystery side
of the communion rail, Barbara's somewhere downstairs,

and I am standing at the rail, letting my arms hang, trying
not to interfere with incarnation. How to match myself

with myself, that good earth? If God were still a woman,
would I keep myself closer to the soil, with its virtues?

I accept that I have written Barbara and Father Andrew
into opposite corners of my heart where they noisily perform

this or that, always on the verge of some sacramental moment.
Yet over and over, beginning and end keep arriving like wine

and blood, silently at the same place. How much building
goes on, to surround it! Yesterday I told my husband:

even if no birds settle in our birdhouse, still we will have tried
to give something back. A nice, peaked house.

Why is it the higher the roof, the more like a church? As if
we could give God's space back, sun and shadow.

Barbara

Today a tooth came loose
from my upper plate and I glued it in
myself, with Superglue, fixed that
little piece of me without
the old panic of falling apart.

DATE DUE